100 Sight Words

This book

belongs to

Introduction to "100 Sight Words"

Welcome to *"100 Sight Words,"* a book designed especially for children who are beginning their journey into reading and writing! The goal of this book is to help kids master the foundational sight words, which are the building blocks of fluent reading and writing in English.

Each page in this book offers engaging and diverse activities, including:

- **Read the word:** Encourages children to recognize words at a glance.
- **Color the word:** Enhances visual memory through creative coloring.
- **Build the word:** Helps kids understand the structure of letters within the word.
- **Clap the syllables:** Develops rhythm and phonological awareness.
- **Trace and write the word:** Builds fine motor skills and reinforces correct spelling.
- **Fill in the missing letter:** Supports spelling and letter recognition.
- **Find and circle the word:** Boosts focus and visual scanning abilities.

These interactive exercises make learning fun and accessible, allowing children to practice essential skills in a friendly and engaging way. Parents and teachers can use this book as a supportive tool for daily learning, inspiring kids to practice consistently.

We believe that *"100 Sight Words"* will be an exciting and joyful guide for children on their educational journey. Grab your pencils, crayons, and enthusiasm – it's time to learn through play!

How to Use This Book

This book is designed to be simple and easy to use for both children and the adults supporting their learning. Here are a few tips on how to make the most of it:

1.   **Daily Practice:** Work with your child on one or two words each day. Regular, short sessions are more effective than longer but infrequent ones.

2.   **Variety of Activities:** Each page includes different exercises to develop reading and writing skills, such as:

Tracing and Writing Words: Helps improve fine motor skills and handwriting precision.

Coloring and Building Words: Strengthens visual memory and engagement.

Finding and Circling Words: Improves focus and word recognition.

3.   **Talk and Play:** Engage your child in conversations about the words they're practicing. Try creating sentences together using new words, or turn learning into a game by incorporating words into daily activities.

4.   **Encourage and Reward:** Celebrate your child's progress, even the small milestones. Use stickers, colorful stamps, or a progress chart to motivate them and make learning fun.

5.   **Review Often:** Regularly revisit previously learned words to help solidify them in your child's memory. Go back to earlier pages to ensure they can still recognize the words confidently.

Remember, every child learns at their own pace. The key is patience, positive reinforcement, and making learning an enjoyable experience. With this book, learning will become an exciting adventure!

Sight Word Practice

Read the word.

the

Color the word.

the

Build the word.

e   h   t

Clap !!!

How many syllables?

1   2   3

Trace the word.

the

Write the word.

Fill in the missing letter.

t_e

Color the letters to make the word.

a   u   m   t   h   e

o   t   h   e   k   z

Find and circle the word.

the   when   come   the   people   the

many   the   the   were   words   have

the   about   way   could   the   each

 # Sight Word Practice 

Read the word.

of

Color the word.

of

Build the word.

f   o

Clap !!!

How many syllables?

(1)   (2)   (3)

Trace the word.

of

Write the word.

Fill in the missing letter.

o__

Color the letters to make the word.

(o) (u) (o) (f) (e) (r)

(f) (x) (v) (w) (o) (f)

Find and circle the word.

of	when	have	of	people	from
other	of	write	were	of	have
down	about	of	could	from	of

Sight Word Practice

Read the word.

and

Color the word.

and

Build the word.

a d n

Clap !!!

How many syllables?

(1) (2) (3)

Trace the word.

and

Write the word.

Fill in the missing letters.

a_ _

Color the letters to make the word.

(p)(a)(n)(d)(e)(r)

(o)(x)(v)(a)(n)(d)

Find and circle the word.

your	and	were	and	people	and
made	said	write	were	and	have
and	about	and	will	from	and

Read the word.	Color the word.
a	a

Build the word.	Clap !!!
a	How many syllables? (1) (2) (3)

Trace the word.	Write the word.
a	

Fill in the missing letter.	Color the letters to make the word.
__	(a) (u) (m) (a) (e) (z) (h) (f) (a) (w) (k) (a)

Find and circle the word.

your	when	a	what	a	not
a	said	write	a	your	have
use	day	a	could	from	a

Sight Word Practice

Read the word.

to

Color the word.

to

Build the word.

o t

Clap !!!

How many syllables?

1   2   3

Trace the word.

to

Write the word.

Fill in the missing letter.

t_

Color the letters to make the word.

g t m t e t
f o v o k o

Find and circle the word.

your	to	way	what	with	can
to	said	to	to	are	to
to	about	them	could	to	each

Sight Word Practice

Read the word.

in

Color the word.

in

Build the word.

n   i

Clap !!!

How many syllables?

(1)   (2)   (3)

Trace the word.

in

Write the word.

Fill in the missing letter.

_n

Color the letters to make the word.

(i) (n) (m) (b) (i) (n)

(h) (x) (i) (n) (k) (z)

Find and circle the word.

your	in	time	in	people	made
then	said	write	were	in	have
in	in	water	could	from	in

 Sight Word Practice 

Read the word.

is

Color the word.

is

Build the word.

s i

Clap !!!

How many syllables?

(1) (2) (3)

Trace the word.

is

Write the word.

Fill in the missing letter.

i_

Color the letters to make the word.

(i) (u) (i) (b) (i) (r)

(s) (x) (s) (w) (s) (z)

Find and circle the word.

your	is	some	what	is	you
have	said	is	were	her	is
is	about	been	is	from	each

 Sight Word Practice 

Read the word.

you

Color the word.

you

Build the word.

u Y o

Clap !!!

How many syllables?

(1) (2) (3)

Trace the word.

you

Write the word.

Fill in the missing letter.

y__u

Color the letters to make the word.

(n) (y) (o) (u) (e) (m)

(k) (a) (v) (y) (o) (u)

Find and circle the word.

see	when	come	you	people	long
you	you	write	were	you	have
down	about	you	could	from	you

Sight Word Practice

Read the word.

that

Color the word.

that

Build the word.

a t t h

Clap !!!

How many syllables?

1 2 3

Trace the word.

that

Write the word.

Fill in the missing letters.

t_a_

Color the letters to make the word.

n u t h a t

t h a t k z

Find and circle the word.

your	when	that	part	people	some
with	that	write	that	number	that
that	about	make	could	that	each

 # Sight Word Practice 

Read the word. it	**Color the word.** it
Build the word. t i	**Clap !!!** How many syllables? 1 2 3
Trace the word. it	**Write the word.**
Fill in the missing letter. _t	**Color the letters to make the word.** i t m b i t h x i t k z

Find and circle the word.

your	it	find	what	than	each
long	said	it	were	it	have
it	about	like	could	from	it

Sight Word Practice

Read the word.

he

Color the word.

he

Build the word.

e h

Clap !!!

How many syllables?

(1) (2) (3)

Trace the word.

he

Write the word.

Fill in the missing letter.

h_

Color the letters to make the word.

(h) (u) (h) (b) (h) (r)

(e) (x) (e) (w) (e) (z)

Find and circle the word.

your	he	been	what	people	did
he	said	write	he	get	he
were	about	he	could	he	each

Sight Word Practice

Read the word.

was

Color the word.

Build the word.

w   s   a

Clap !!!

How many syllables?

(1)   (2)   (3)

Trace the word.

was

Write the word.

Fill in the missing letters.

__a__

Color the letters to make the word.

(n) (w) (a) (s) (e) (r)

(p) (c) (v) (w) (a) (s)

Find and circle the word.

your	was	look	what	was	about
write	said	was	were	long	have
was	was	find	could	from	was

Sight Word Practice

Read the word.

for

Color the word.

for

Build the word.

r   o   f

Clap !!!

How many syllables?

(1)   (2)   (3)

Trace the word.

for

Write the word.

Fill in the missing letters.

f __ __

Color the letters to make the word.

(n) (u) (f) (o) (r) (h)

(f) (o) (r) (w) (k) (z)

Find and circle the word.

but	when	for	what	time	for
for	said	write	were	for	him
not	about	for	could	from	each

 # Sight Word Practice 

Read the word.

on

Color the word.

on

Build the word.

n   o

Clap !!!

How many syllables?

(1)   (2)   (3)

Trace the word.

on

Write the word.

Fill in the missing letter.

o__

Color the letters to make the word.

(o) (n) (m) (b) (o) (n)

(h) (x) (o) (n) (k) (z)

Find and circle the word.

on	when	at	on	part	may
this	on	write	were	on	have
down	about	on	could	from	on

Sight Word Practice

Read the word.

are

Color the word.

are

Build the word.

e   r   a

Clap !!!

How many syllables?

(1)   (2)   (3)

Trace the word.

are

Write the word.

Fill in the missing letters.

_ r _

Color the letters to make the word.

(a) (r) (e) (b) (z) (m)

(h) (x) (v) (a) (r) (e)

Find and circle the word.

are	are	first	what	are	who
can	said	are	were	been	have
and	about	this	are	from	are

 Sight Word Practice 

Read the word.

a s

Color the word.

as

Build the word.

s   a

Clap !!!

How many syllables?

(1)   (2)   (3)

Trace the word.

as

Write the word.

Fill in the missing letter.

a__

Color the letters to make the word.

(l) (a) (m) (a) (e) (a)
(c) (s) (v) (s) (k) (s)

Find and circle the word.

your	when	as	what	into	like
as	as	write	were	as	as
down	about	him	as	from	each

Sight Word Practice

Read the word.

with

Color the word.

with

Build the word.

i   h   t   w

Clap !!!

How many syllables?

(1)   (2)   (3)

Trace the word.

with

Write the word.

Fill in the missing letters.

w_t_

Color the letters to make the word.

(w) (i) (t) (h) (e) (r)

(g) (x) (w) (i) (t) (h)

Find and circle the word.

with	with	they	what	with	more
some	said	with	were	that	have
down	with	part	could	from	with

Sight Word Practice

Read the word.

his

Color the word.

his

Build the word.

s h i

Clap !!!

How many syllables?

(1) (2) (3)

Trace the word.

his

Write the word.

Fill in the missing letters.

h__ __

Color the letters to make the word.

(n) (u) (m) (h) (i) (s)

(h) (i) (s) (w) (k) (z)

Find and circle the word.

your	his	will	his	like	your
not	said	write	were	his	did
his	about	his	could	from	his

Sight Word Practice

Read the word.

they

Color the word.

they

Build the word.

e y h t

Clap !!!

How many syllables?

(1) (2) (3)

Trace the word.

they

Write the word.

Fill in the missing letters.

t_e_

Color the letters to make the word.

(t)(h)(e)(y)(p)(r)
(h)(x)(t)(h)(e)(y)

Find and circle the word.

get	when	they	what	had	they
they	said	write	were	they	have
one	about	they	could	from	each

 # Sight Word Practice 

Read the word.

I

Color the word.

I

Build the word.

I

Clap !!!

How many syllables?

(1) (2) (3)

Trace the word.

I

Write the word.

Fill in the missing letter.

__

Color the letters to make the word.

(I) (u) (m) (I) (e) (r)

(h) (x) (I) (w) (k) (I)

Find and circle the word.

your	when	I	what	been	I
I	said	write	were	use	have
down	come	like	I	from	I

Sight Word Practice

Read the word.

at

Color the word.

at

Build the word.

t   a

Clap !!!

How many syllables?

(1)   (2)   (3)

Trace the word.

at

Write the word.

Fill in the missing letter.

a__

Color the letters to make the word.

(a) (u) (a) (t) (e) (r)

(t) (x) (v) (w) (a) (t)

Find and circle the word.

at	when	at	what	more	at
will	said	write	at	see	have
down	at	can	could	from	at

 # Sight Word Practice 

Read the word.

be

Color the word.

be

Build the word.

e b

Clap !!!

How many syllables?

(1) (2) (3)

Trace the word.

be

Write the word.

Fill in the missing letter.

b＿

Color the letters to make the word.

(b) (e) (m) (r) (b) (e)

(h) (x) (b) (e) (k) (z)

Find and circle the word.

your	be	then	what	may	be
be	said	be	be	write	have
be	can	out	could	be	each

 Sight Word Practice 

Read the word.

this

Color the word.

this

Build the word.

h   s   t   i

Clap !!!

How many syllables?

(1)   (2)   (3)

Trace the word.

this

Write the word.

Fill in the missing letters.

t_i_

Color the letters to make the word.

(x) (u) (m) (f) (e) (r)

(a) (t) (h) (i) (s) (z)

Find and circle the word.

this	when	made	what	first	this
number	this	write	were	this	have
more	about	them	this	from	each

 # Sight Word Practice 

Read the word.

have

Color the word.

have

Build the word.

a h e v

Clap !!!

How many syllables?

(1)   (2)   (3)

Trace the word.

have

Write the word.

Fill in the missing letters.

h_v_

Color the letters to make the word.

(n)(u)(h)(a)(v)(e)

(h)(a)(v)(e)(k)(z)

Find and circle the word.

your	have	have	what	people	make
have	said	write	have	some	have
down	about	have	could	have	each

Sight Word Practice

Read the word.

from

Color the word.

from

Build the word.

m   o   r   f

Clap !!!

How many syllables?

(1)   (2)   (3)

Trace the word.

from

Write the word.

Fill in the missing letters.

f__o__

Color the letters to make the word.

(n) (u) (c) (b) (e) (i)

(h) (f) (r) (o) (m) (z)

Find and circle the word.

from	when	long	what	people	from
come	from	write	from	words	have
down	about	there	could	from	each

 # Sight Word Practice 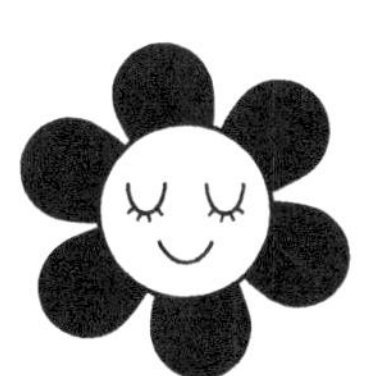

Read the word.

or

Color the word.

or

Build the word.

r   o

Clap !!!

How many syllables?

(1)   (2)   (3)

Trace the word.

or

Write the word.

Fill in the missing letter.

o__

Color the letters to make the word.

(o) (r) (m) (b) (o) (r)

(h) (x) (o) (r) (k) (z)

Find and circle the word.

your	or	made	or	water	then
or	said	write	were	or	have
way	about	or	could	from	or

Sight Word Practice

Read the word.

one

Color the word.

one

Build the word.

e   n   o

Clap !!!

How many syllables?

1   2   3

Trace the word.

one

Write the word.

Fill in the missing letters.

_n_

Color the letters to make the word.

Find and circle the word.

your	when	one	what	one	them
one	said	write	were	part	have
down	one	some	one	from	one

 Sight Word Practice 

Read the word.

had

Color the word.

had

Build the word.

a d h

Clap !!!

How many syllables?

(1)   (2)   (3)

Trace the word.

had

Write the word.

Fill in the missing letter.

h_d

Color the letters to make the word.

(n) (h) (a) (d) (e) (r)

(o) (x) (v) (h) (a) (d)

Find and circle the word.

your	when	had	what	had	was
had	said	write	were	with	have
are	had	number	had	from	had

 Sight Word Practice 

Read the word.

by

Color the word.

by

Build the word.

y   b

Clap !!!

How many syllables?

1   2   3

Trace the word.

by

Write the word.

Fill in the missing letter.

b__

Color the letters to make the word.

b u m b e r

y x v y k z

Find and circle the word.

your	by	who	what	by	two
by	said	write	by	her	have
its	about	by	could	from	by

 # Sight Word Practice 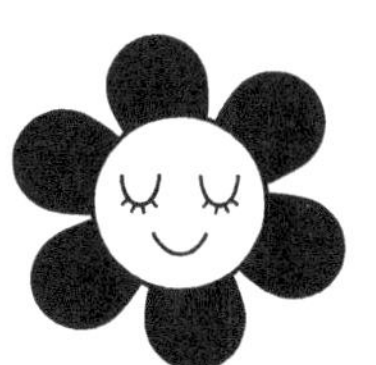

Read the word.

words

Color the word.

Build the word.

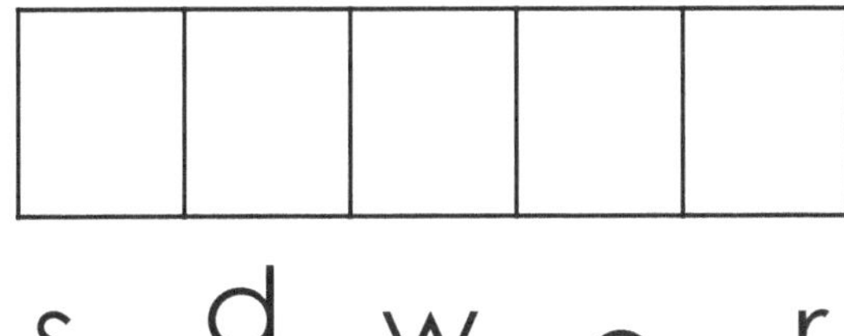

Clap !!!

How many syllables?

 1    2    3

Trace the word.

words

Write the word.

Fill in the missing letters.

w__r__s

Color the letters to make the word.

 e    u    j    b    e    v

h   w   o   r   d   s

Find and circle the word.

words	when	these	what	words	have
make	words	write	words	first	words
down	about	words	could	from	each

Sight Word Practice

Read the word.

but

Color the word.

but

Build the word.

t b u

Clap !!!

How many syllables?

(1)   (2)   (3)

Trace the word.

but

Write the word.

Fill in the missing letters.

b __ __

Color the letters to make the word.

(n) (u) (b) (u) (t) (r)

(b) (u) (t) (w) (k) (z)

Find and circle the word.

your	when	been	what	but	but
then	but	write	were	long	have
down	about	but	but	from	each

 Sight Word Practice 

Read the word.

not

Color the word.

not

Build the word.

o t n

Clap !!!

How many syllables?

(1)   (2)   (3)

Trace the word.

not

Write the word.

Fill in the missing letter.

n_t

Color the letters to make the word.

(n) (o) (t) (b) (e) (r)

(h) (x) (v) (n) (o) (t)

Find and circle the word.

your	not	who	not	people	with
not	said	write	were	not	have
down	day	not	could	from	not

Sight Word Practice

Read the word.

what

Color the word.

what

Build the word.

t   w   a   h

Clap !!!

How many syllables?

(1)   (2)   (3)

Trace the word.

what

Write the word.

Fill in the missing letters.

w__a__

Color the letters to make the word.

(n) (u) (c) (b) (e) (r)

(o) (x) (w) (h) (a) (t)

Find and circle the word.

what	when	what	see	people	what
look	said	write	what	called	have
down	what	some	could	what	each

 Sight Word Practice 

Read the word.

all

Color the word.

all

Build the word.

| l | a | l |

Clap !!!

How many syllables?

(1)   (2)   (3)

Trace the word.

all

Write the word.

Fill in the missing letters.

a__ __

Color the letters to make the word.

(f) (a) (l) (l) (e) (r)

(h) (x) (v) (a) (l) (l)

Find and circle the word.

all	when	did	what	all	my
get	all	write	all	way	all
down	about	all	could	from	each

Sight Word Practice

Read the word.

were

Color the word.

were

Build the word.

e   w   e   r

Clap !!!

How many syllables?

(1)   (2)   (3)

Trace the word.

were

Write the word.

Fill in the missing letters.

w_r_

Color the letters to make the word.

(o) (w) (e) (r) (e) (p)

(h) (x) (v) (t) (k) (z)

Find and circle the word.

were	when	were	what	each	would
other	were	write	were	were	have
were	about	these	were	from	were

Sight Word Practice

Read the word.

we

Color the word.

we

Build the word.

e   w

Clap !!!

How many syllables?

(1)   (2)   (3)

Trace the word.

we

Write the word.

Fill in the missing letter.

w__

Color the letters to make the word.

(n) (w) (e) (b) (p) (r)

(h) (x) (v) (w) (e) (z)

Find and circle the word.

your	when	we	we	people	words
we	said	write	were	we	have
down	we	about	could	from	we

Sight Word Practice

Read the word.

when

Color the word.

when

Build the word.

n h e w

Clap !!!

How many syllables?

1 2 3

Trace the word.

when

Write the word.

Fill in the missing letters.

w_e_

Color the letters to make the word.

g u m b f r

l w h e n z

Find and circle the word.

your	when	made	what	when	other
when	said	write	were	them	have
down	about	when	could	from	when

Sight Word Practice

Read the word.

your

Color the word.

your

Build the word.

u Y r o

Clap !!!

How many syllables?

(1) (2) (3)

Trace the word.

your

Write the word.

Fill in the missing letters.

y__u__

Color the letters to make the word.

(y)(o)(u)(r)(e)(j)

(h)(x)(y)(o)(u)(r)

Find and circle the word.

your	when	your	what	people	time
like	your	write	were	your	have
your	about	down	your	from	your

Sight Word Practice

Read the word.

can

Color the word.

can

Build the word.

n a c

Clap !!!

How many syllables?

(1) (2) (3)

Trace the word.

can

Write the word.

Fill in the missing letter.

c_n

Color the letters to make the word.

(c) (a) (n) (b) (e) (r)

(h) (x) (c) (a) (n) (z)

Find and circle the word.

your	can	first	what	can	can
some	said	can	were	other	have
can	about	than	can	from	each

Sight Word Practice

Read the word.

said

Color the word.

said

Build the word.

i   d   a   s

Clap !!!

How many syllables?

(1)   (2)   (3)

Trace the word.

said

Write the word.

Fill in the missing letters.

s__i__

Color the letters to make the word.

(n) (u) (m) (o) (e) (r)

(s) (a) (i) (d) (k) (z)

Find and circle the word.

said	when	look	said	people	other
water	said	write	were	said	have
down	about	said	could	from	said

Sight Word Practice

Read the word.

there

Color the word.

there

Build the word.

e   h   e   t   r

Clap !!!

How many syllables?

(1)   (2)   (3)

Trace the word.

there

Write the word.

Fill in the missing letters.

th_r_

Color the letters to make the word.

(g) (u) (m) (b) (f) (v)

(p) (t) (h) (e) (r) (e)

Find and circle the word.

your	when	there	what	people	there
there	said	write	were	there	have
down	about	there	could	from	each

# Sight Word Practice 

Read the word.

use

Color the word.

use

Build the word.

e u s

Clap !!!

How many syllables?

(1) (2) (3)

Trace the word.

use

Write the word.

Fill in the missing letters.

u _ _

Color the letters to make the word.

(n)(p)(m)(u)(s)(e)
(u)(s)(e)(w)(k)(z)

Find and circle the word.

use	when	are	what	use	for
more	use	use	were	them	use
down	about	some	could	use	each

Sight Word Practice

Read the word.

a n

Color the word.

an

Build the word.

n a

Clap !!!

How many syllables?

(1) (2) (3)

Trace the word.

an

Write the word.

Fill in the missing letter.

a__

Color the letters to make the word.

(a)(u)(a)(b)(a)(r)

(n)(x)(n)(w)(n)(z)

Find and circle the word.

your	an	did	an	people	an
an	said	write	were	an	have
down	about	an	get	from	an

 # Sight Word Practice 

Read the word.

each

Color the word.

Build the word.

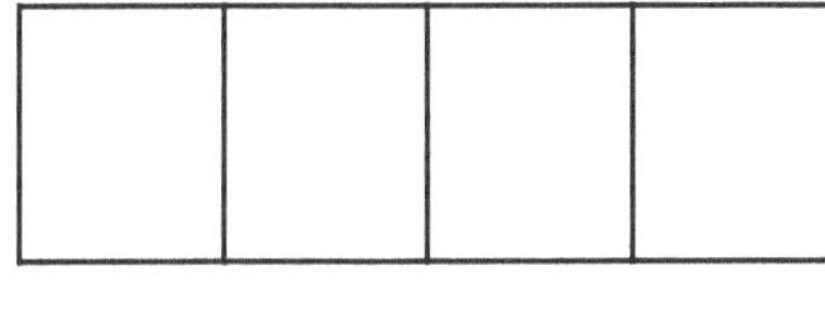

h a c e

Clap !!!

How many syllables?

1   2   3

Trace the word.

Write the word.

Fill in the missing letters.

e__ __h

Color the letters to make the word.

n   u   m   b   f   r

g   e   a   c   h   z

Find and circle the word.

your	when	each	what	each	look
each	said	write	each	come	have
each	about	each	could	from	each

Sight Word Practice

Read the word.

which

Color the word.

which

Build the word.

i h w h c

Clap !!!

How many syllables?

(1) (2) (3)

Trace the word.

which

Write the word.

Fill in the missing letters.

wh__c__

Color the letters to make the word.

(n) (w) (h) (i) (c) (h)
(g) (x) (v) (t) (k) (z)

Find and circle the word.

your	when	which	what	their	which
which	said	write	which	been	have
down	which	first	could	which	each

 # Sight Word Practice 

Read the word.

she

Color the word.

she

Build the word.

e s h

Clap !!!

How many syllables?

(1) (2) (3)

Trace the word.

she

Write the word.

Fill in the missing letter.

s__e

Color the letters to make the word.

(n) (u) (m) (s) (h) (e)

(s) (h) (e) (w) (k) (z)

Find and circle the word.

your	when	she	what	people	she
she	said	write	she	many	have
made	she	how	could	she	each

Sight Word Practice

Read the word.

do

Color the word.

do

Build the word.

o   d

Clap !!!

How many syllables?

(1)   (2)   (3)

Trace the word.

do

Write the word.

Fill in the missing letter.

d_

Color the letters to make the word.

(n) (d) (m) (d) (e) (d)

(h) (o) (v) (o) (k) (o)

Find and circle the word.

your	do	called	what	do	words
many	said	do	were	may	have
do	about	write	do	from	do

 # Sight Word Practice 

Read the word.

how

Color the word.

how

Build the word.

o   h   w

Clap !!!

How many syllables?

(1)   (2)   (3)

Trace the word.

how

Write the word.

Fill in the missing letters.

h_ _

Color the letters to make the word.

(n) (u) (h) (o) (w) (r)

(h) (o) (w) (j) (k) (z)

Find and circle the word.

how	when	how	what	people	other
your	how	write	how	long	how
down	about	how	could	how	each

Sight Word Practice

Read the word.

their

Color the word.

their

Build the word.

e   i   t   r   h

Clap !!!

How many syllables?

(1)   (2)   (3)

Trace the word.

their

Write the word.

Fill in the missing letters.

th__ __r

Color the letters to make the word.

(d) (u) (m) (b) (f) (o)

(g) (t) (h) (e) (i) (r)

Find and circle the word.

your	their	some	what	people	their
their	said	write	their	find	have
their	about	their	could	their	each

 # Sight Word Practice 

Read the word.

if

Color the word.

if

Build the word.

f   i

Clap !!!

How many syllables?

(1)   (2)   (3)

Trace the word.

if

Write the word.

Fill in the missing letter.

i__

Color the letters to make the word.

(i) (u) (i) (b) (i) (r)
(f) (x) (f) (w) (f) (z)

Find and circle the word.

if	when	if	if	am	did
get	if	write	were	if	have
down	if	its	them	from	if

Sight Word Practice

Read the word.

will

Color the word.

Build the word.

l W l i

Clap !!!

How many syllables?

(1) (2) (3)

Trace the word.

will

Write the word.

Fill in the missing letters.

W__ __ l

Color the letters to make the word.

(w) (i) (l) (l) (e) (r)

(h) (x) (v) (g) (k) (z)

Find and circle the word.

your	will	with	what	will	had
will	said	will	were	write	will
down	about	more	will	from	each

Sight Word Practice

Read the word.

up

Color the word.

up

Build the word.

p   U

Clap !!!

How many syllables?

(1)   (2)   (3)

Trace the word.

up

Write the word.

Fill in the missing letter.

U__

Color the letters to make the word.

(u) (p) (m) (b) (u) (p)

(h) (x) (u) (p) (k) (z)

Find and circle the word.

up	up	into	up	use	time
see	said	write	were	up	have
up	about	up	up	from	up

Sight Word Practice

Read the word.

other

Color the word.

other

Build the word.

t e h o r

Clap !!!

How many syllables?

(1) (2) (3)

Trace the word.

other

Write the word.

Fill in the missing letters.

o_h_r

Color the letters to make the word.

(n) (u) (m) (b) (f) (g)

(g) (o) (t) (h) (e) (r)

Find and circle the word.

other	when	made	what	people	other
first	other	write	other	called	have
down	about	other	could	other	each

 # Sight Word Practice 

Read the word.

about

Color the word.

Build the word.

a   o   t   b   u

Clap !!!

How many syllables?

 1    2   3

Trace the word.

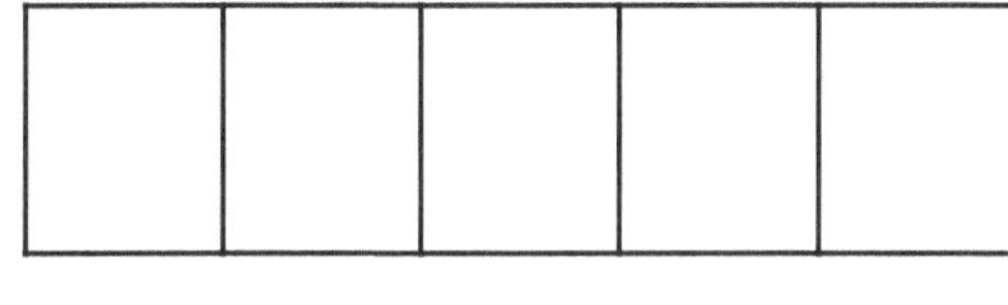

Write the word.

Fill in the missing letters.

a__o__t

Color the letters to make the word.

 n    a    b    o    u    t

 h    x    v    w   k   z

Find and circle the word.

about	when	all	what	people	write
more	said	about	were	about	have
down	about	number	could	from	about

Sight Word Practice

Read the word.

out

Color the word.

out

Build the word.

t u o

Clap !!!

How many syllables?

(1)   (2)   (3)

Trace the word.

out

Write the word.

Fill in the missing letters.

o__ __

Color the letters to make the word.

(n) (o) (u) (t) (e) (r)

(h) (x) (v) (o) (u) (t)

Find and circle the word.

your	when	out	what	people	out
out	said	write	were	out	have
down	about	out	could	from	each

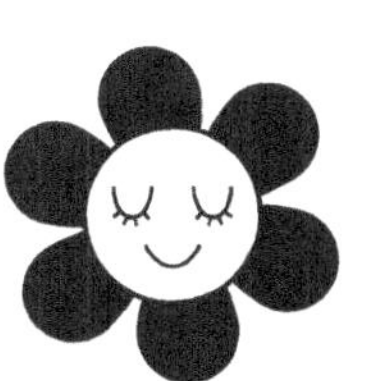

Sight Word Practice

Read the word.

many

Color the word.

Build the word.

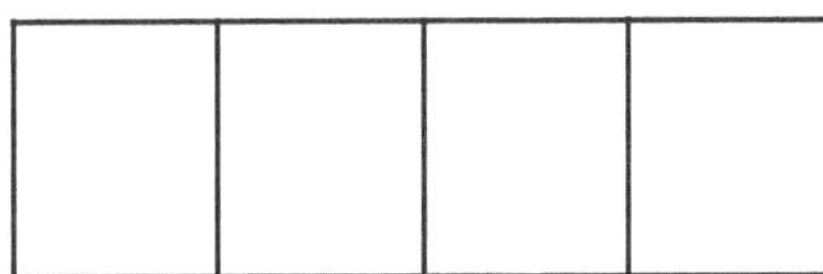

n   y   a   m

Clap !!!

How many syllables?

(1)   (2)   (3)

Trace the word.

many

Write the word.

Fill in the missing letters.

m__ __y

Color the letters to make the word.

(m) (a) (n) (y) (e) (r)

(h) (x) (v) (w) (k) (z)

Find and circle the word.

your	when	many	what	people	many
many	said	write	many	number	have
down	many	words	could	many	each

 Sight Word Practice 

Read the word.

then

Color the word.

then

Build the word.

e   n   h   t

Clap !!!

How many syllables?

(1)   (2)   (3)

Trace the word.

then

Write the word.

Fill in the missing letters.

t__ __n

Color the letters to make the word.

(t) (h) (e) (n) (j) (r)

(g) (x) (t) (h) (e) (n)

Find and circle the word.

your	then	your	what	people	then
then	said	then	were	then	have
down	about	find	then	from	each

Sight Word Practice

Read the word.

them

Color the word.

them

Build the word.

e h t m

Clap !!!

How many syllables?

(1) (2) (3)

Trace the word.

them

Write the word.

Fill in the missing letters.

th__ __

Color the letters to make the word.

(n) (u) (o) (b) (u) (r)

(d) (t) (h) (e) (m) (z)

Find and circle the word.

them	when	them	what	people	their
some	them	write	them	these	have
down	them	number	could	them	them

Sight Word Practice

Read the word.

these

Color the word.

these

Build the word.

e   s   e   t   h

Clap !!!

How many syllables?

1   2   3

Trace the word.

these

Write the word.

Fill in the missing letters.

th__s__

Color the letters to make the word.

n u m b g r

f t h e s e

Find and circle the word.

your	these	been	what	people	these
first	said	these	were	these	have
these	about	than	these	from	each

 # Sight Word Practice 

Read the word.

so

Color the word.

so

Build the word.

o   s

Clap !!!

How many syllables?

(1)   (2)   (3)

Trace the word.

so

Write the word.

Fill in the missing letter.

s___

Color the letters to make the word.

(n) (s) (m) (s) (e) (s)

(h) (o) (v) (o) (k) (o)

Find and circle the word.

your	when	so	what	long	so
so	said	write	so	words	have
down	so	him	could	so	each

Sight Word Practice

Read the word.

some

Color the word.

some

Build the word.

e s m o

Clap !!!

How many syllables?

1 2 3

Trace the word.

some

Write the word.

Fill in the missing letters.

s__ __e

Color the letters to make the word.

n s o m e r
h x v w k z

Find and circle the word.

your	when	said	what	some	write
some	said	some	were	these	have
down	some	them	some	from	some

 # Sight Word Practice 

Read the word.

her

Color the word.

her

Build the word.

e　h　r

Clap !!!

How many syllables?

(1)　(2)　(3)

Trace the word.

her

Write the word.

Fill in the missing letter.

h_r

Color the letters to make the word.

(h) (e) (r) (b) (f) (g)

(p) (x) (v) (h) (e) (r)

Find and circle the word.

been	her	number	her	water	would
her	said	write	were	her	have
down	about	her	could	from	her

 # Sight Word Practice 

Read the word.

would

Color the word.

would

Build the word.

d w l o u

Clap !!!

How many syllables?

1 2 3

Trace the word.

would

Write the word.

Fill in the missing letters.

w__u__d

Color the letters to make the word.

n a m b e r

h w o u l d

Find and circle the word.

would	when	would	what	would	find
these	would	write	would	them	have
would	about	would	long	from	would

Sight Word Practice

Read the word.

make

Color the word.

make

Build the word.

a   e   m   k

Clap !!!

How many syllables?

(1)   (2)   (3)

Trace the word.

make

Write the word.

Fill in the missing letters.

m__k__

Color the letters to make the word.

(n) (u) (g) (b) (f) (r)
(h) (m) (a) (k) (e) (z)

Find and circle the word.

make	when	many	what	make	each
had	make	write	make	time	make
down	about	make	could	from	each

 # Sight Word Practice 

Read the word.

like

Color the word.

like

Build the word.

i k l e

Clap !!!

How many syllables?

(1)   (2)   (3)

Trace the word.

like

Write the word.

Fill in the missing letters.

l_k_

Color the letters to make the word.

(l) (i) (k) (e) (y) (r)

(h) (x) (v) (w) (k) (z)

Find and circle the word.

your	like	your	what	way	like
that	said	like	were	like	have
like	about	part	could	from	each

 # Sight Word Practice 

Read the word.

him

Color the word.

him

Build the word.

i h m

Clap !!!

How many syllables?

1   2   3

Trace the word.

him

Write the word.

Fill in the missing letters.

h__ __

Color the letters to make the word.

h i m b e r

g x v h i m

Find and circle the word.

your	him	but	what	him	one
him	said	write	him	day	him
down	did	him	could	from	each

 # Sight Word Practice 

Read the word.

into

Color the word.

into

Build the word.

t i n o

Clap !!!

How many syllables?

(1) (2) (3)

Trace the word.

into

Write the word.

Fill in the missing letters.

in___ __

Color the letters to make the word.

(k) (u) (m) (b) (e) (r)

(h) (x) (i) (n) (t) (o)

Find and circle the word.

your	into	time	what	use	into
into	said	into	into	other	have
down	about	when	could	into	each

 # Sight Word Practice 

Read the word.

time

Color the word.

Build the word.

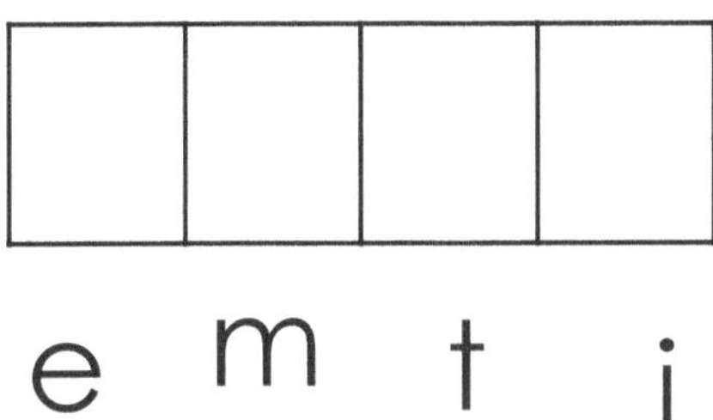

e m t i

Clap !!!

How many syllables?

 1  2  3

Trace the word.

Write the word.

Fill in the missing letters.

t_m__

Color the letters to make the word.

   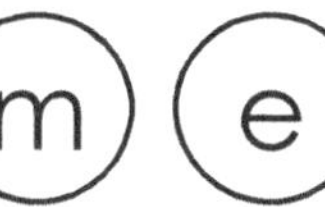

Find and circle the word.

your	time	other	what	people	time
down	said	time	were	time	have
time	about	words	time	from	each

Sight Word Practice

Read the word.

has

Color the word.

has

Build the word.

s   h   a

Clap !!!

How many syllables?

(1)   (2)   (3)

Trace the word.

has

Write the word.

Fill in the missing letters.

h___ ___

Color the letters to make the word.

(h) (a) (s) (b) (e) (r)

(c) (x) (v) (h) (a) (s)

Find and circle the word.

your	has	find	has	people	long
has	said	has	were	has	have
down	has	into	has	from	has

 Sight Word Practice 

Read the word.

look

Color the word.

look

Build the word.

o   l   o   k

Clap !!!

How many syllables?

1   2   3

Trace the word.

look

Write the word.

Fill in the missing letters.

l__ __k

Color the letters to make the word.

n u m b e r

h l o o k z

Find and circle the word.

your	when	look	what	people	come
look	said	write	look	there	look
down	look	have	could	look	each

Sight Word Practice

Read the word.

two

Color the word.

two

Build the word.

w t o

Clap !!!

How many syllables?

1   2   3

Trace the word.

two

Write the word.

Fill in the missing letters.

t _ _

Color the letters to make the word.

t w o b e r

h x v t w o

Find and circle the word.

your	when	two	what	long	two
two	said	write	two	like	have
down	two	time	could	two	each

Sight Word Practice

Read the word.

more

Color the word.

Build the word.

e   r   m   o

Clap !!!

How many syllables?

1   2   3

Trace the word.

more

Write the word.

Fill in the missing letters.

m__r__

Color the letters to make the word.

n u k b f g

h x m o r e

Find and circle the word.

your	when	come	more	people	can
said	more	write	were	more	have
more	about	more	could	from	more

 Sight Word Practice 

Read the word.

write

Color the word.

write

Build the word.

i w e r t

Clap !!!

How many syllables?

(1)   (2)   (3)

Trace the word.

write

Write the word.

Fill in the missing letters.

w_i_e

Color the letters to make the word.

(w) (r) (i) (t) (e) (k)
(h) (x) (v) (p) (s) (z)

Find and circle the word.

your	when	number	write	first	how
write	said	write	were	write	have
time	write	their	could	from	write

 Sight Word Practice 

Read the word.

go

Color the word.

go

Build the word.

o g

Clap !!!

How many syllables?

(1) (2) (3)

Trace the word.

go

Write the word.

Fill in the missing letter.

g__

Color the letters to make the word.

(g) (u) (g) (b) (g) (r)

(o) (x) (o) (w) (o) (z)

Find and circle the word.

go	when	go	what	people	go
first	said	write	go	all	have
down	go	then	could	go	each

Sight Word Practice

Read the word.

see

Color the word.

see

Build the word.

e   s   e

Clap !!!

How many syllables?

1   2   3

Trace the word.

see

Write the word.

Fill in the missing letters.

s___ ___

Color the letters to make the word.

n   u   m   s   e   e

s   e   e   w   k   z

Find and circle the word.

your	see	her	what	now	see
see	said	see	were	see	have
down	about	find	see	from	each

 Sight Word Practice 

Read the word.	Color the word.
number	number

Build the word.

e u m b n r

Clap !!!

How many syllables?

(1) (2) (3)

Trace the word.

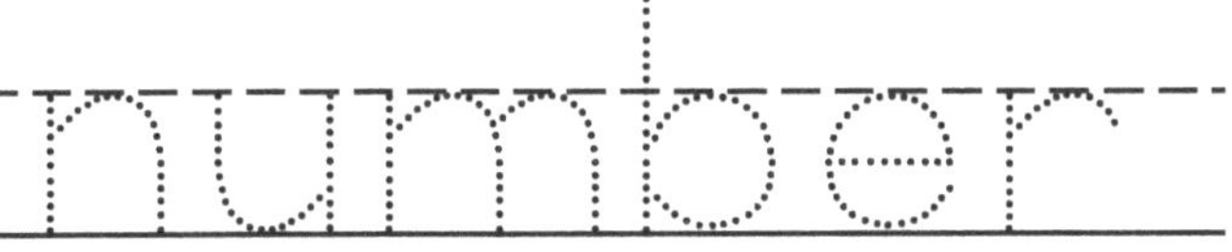 number

Write the word.

Fill in the missing letters.

n__m__er

Color the letters to make the word.

(n) (u) (m) (b) (e) (r)

(h) (x) (v) (w) (k) (z)

Find and circle the word.

your	when	number	what	people	number
number	said	write	were	number	have
down	about	number	could	from	each

 # Sight Word Practice 

Read the word.

no

Color the word.

no

Build the word.

o   n

Clap !!!

How many syllables?

(1)   (2)   (3)

Trace the word.

no

Write the word.

Fill in the missing letter.

n__

Color the letters to make the word.

(n) (j) (r) (n) (e) (n)

(o) (x) (v) (o) (k) (o)

Find and circle the word.

your	when	no	what	her	are
way	no	write	no	its	no
no	about	out	could	no	each

 # Sight Word Practice 

Read the word.

way

Color the word.

way

Build the word.

a y w

Clap !!!

How many syllables?

(1)   (2)   (3)

Trace the word.

way

Write the word.

Fill in the missing letters.

w__ __

Color the letters to make the word.

(n) (w) (a) (y) (e) (r)

(f) (x) (v) (w) (a) (y)

Find and circle the word.

way	when	way	what	people	way
long	way	write	way	how	have
down	about	them	could	way	each

 # Sight Word Practice 

Read the word.

could

Color the word.

could

Build the word.

l   U   c   d   o

Clap !!!

How many syllables?

(1)   (2)   (3)

Trace the word.

could

Write the word.

Fill in the missing letters.

c __ u __ d

Color the letters to make the word.

(c) (o) (u) (l) (d) (r)

(h) (x) (v) (w) (k) (z)

Find and circle the word.

your	could	some	what	could	water
could	said	could	were	make	could
down	could	them	could	from	each

Sight Word Practice

Read the word. **people**	Color the word. people
Build the word. p l e p e o	Clap !!! How many syllables? 1 2 3
Trace the word. people	Write the word.
Fill in the missing letters. p__op__e	Color the letters to make the word. n u k b g r p e o p l e

Find and circle the word.

people	when	number	what	people	called
which	people	write	people	there	have
down	about	words	could	from	people

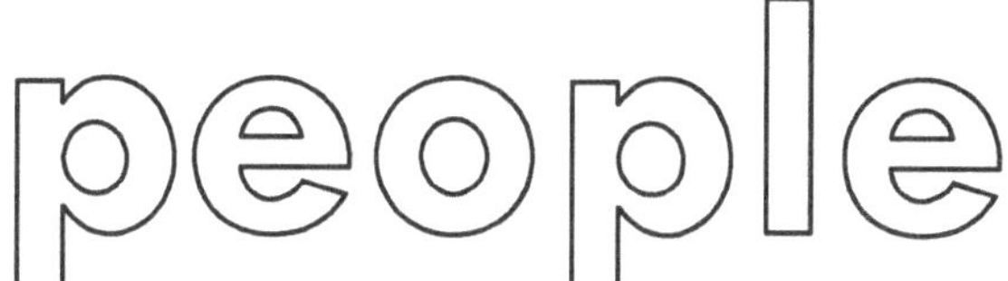

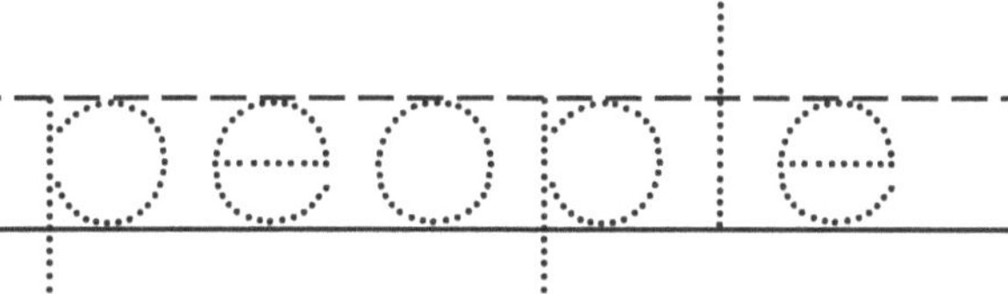

 # Sight Word Practice 

Read the word.

my

Color the word.

my

Build the word.

y   m

Clap !!!

How many syllables?

(1)   (2)   (3)

Trace the word.

my

Write the word.

Fill in the missing letter.

m__

Color the letters to make the word.

(a) (m) (k) (m) (e) (m)
(h) (y) (v) (y) (k) (y)

Find and circle the word.

my	when	my	what	other	my
made	my	write	my	first	have
down	about	them	could	my	each

Sight Word Practice

Read the word.

than

Color the word.

than

Build the word.

n t a h

Clap !!!

How many syllables?

(1) (2) (3)

Trace the word.

than

Write the word.

Fill in the missing letters.

t_a_

Color the letters to make the word.

(n)(u)(y)(b)(e)(r)
(t)(h)(a)(n)(k)(z)

Find and circle the word.

your	when	than	what	people	than
than	said	write	than	into	have
down	than	time	could	than	each

Sight Word Practice

Read the word.	Color the word.
first	first

Build the word.

i   r   f   t   s

Clap !!!

How many syllables?

(1)   (2)   (3)

Trace the word.

first

Write the word.

Fill in the missing letters.

f_ _r_ _t

Color the letters to make the word.

(f) (i) (r) (s) (t) (o)
(h) (x) (v) (w) (k) (z)

Find and circle the word.

first	when	come	first	more	look
long	said	first	were	first	have
down	first	like	could	from	first

 # Sight Word Practice 

Read the word.

water

Color the word.

Build the word.

Clap !!!

How many syllables?

1   2   3

Trace the word.

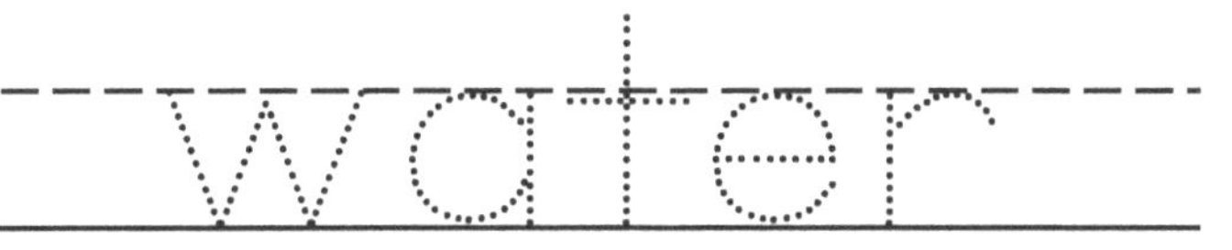

Write the word.

Fill in the missing letters.

w__ __er

Color the letters to make the word.

Find and circle the word.

them	when	water	what	called	water
water	said	write	were	water	have
down	about	water	could	from	each

Sight Word Practice

Read the word.

been

Color the word.

been

Build the word.

e n e b

Clap !!!

How many syllables?

1 2 3

Trace the word.

been

Write the word.

Fill in the missing letters.

b__ __n

Color the letters to make the word.

f u b e e n
h x v w k z

Find and circle the word.

your	when	this	what	been	like
come	been	been	were	number	been
been	about	long	been	from	each

Sight Word Practice

Read the word.

called

Color the word.

Build the word.

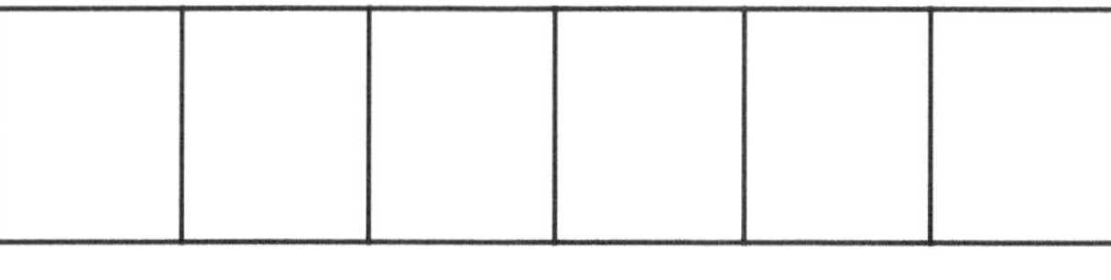

Clap !!!

How many syllables?

(1)   (2)   (3)

Trace the word.

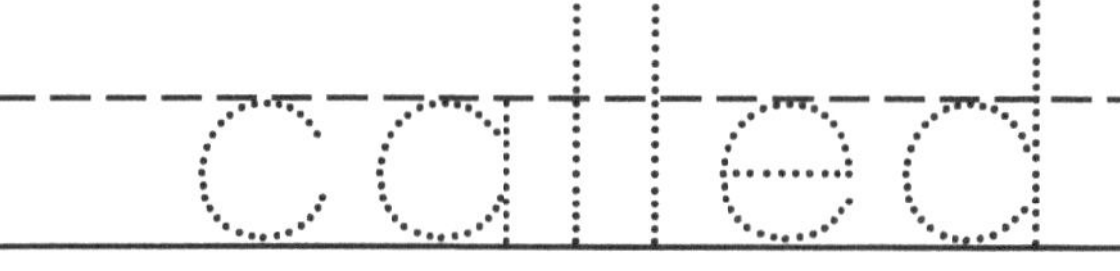

Write the word.

Fill in the missing letters.

c__ll__d

Color the letters to make the word.

(c) (a) (l) (l) (e) (d)
(h) (x) (v) (w) (k) (z)

Find and circle the word.

called	when	look	what	people	called
water	said	called	called	more	have
down	called	some	could	from	called

Sight Word Practice

Read the word.

who

Color the word.

who

Build the word.

h   w   o

Clap !!!

How many syllables?

(1)   (2)   (3)

Trace the word.

who

Write the word.

Fill in the missing letter.

w__o

Color the letters to make the word.

(n) (u) (y) (w) (h) (o)

(w) (h) (o) (j) (k) (z)

Find and circle the word.

your	when	about	what	who	look
who	said	who	were	other	who
down	who	than	who	from	each

 # Sight Word Practice 

Read the word.

a m

Color the word.

am

Build the word.

m a

Clap !!!

How many syllables?

(1)   (2)   (3)

Trace the word.

am

Write the word.

Fill in the missing letter.

a__

Color the letters to make the word.

(a) (m) (k) (a) (e) (a)

(h) (x) (v) (m) (f) (m)

Find and circle the word.

your	am	make	what	am	two
find	said	am	were	long	am
am	about	look	am	from	each

Sight Word Practice

Read the word.

its

Color the word.

its

Build the word.

t   i   s

Clap !!!

How many syllables?

1   2   3

Trace the word.

its

Write the word.

Fill in the missing letters.

i__ __

Color the letters to make the word.

i t s b e r

h x v i t s

Find and circle the word.

your	when	its	what	people	its
its	said	write	were	its	have
down	about	its	could	from	each

Sight Word Practice

Read the word.

now

Color the word.

now

Build the word.

o   n   w

Clap !!!

How many syllables?

(1)   (2)   (3)

Trace the word.

now

Write the word.

Fill in the missing letters.

n__ __

Color the letters to make the word.

(n) (o) (w) (b) (e) (r)

(h) (x) (v) (n) (o) (w)

Find and circle the word.

your	when	other	now	people	there
now	said	now	were	made	now
down	now	words	now	from	each

Sight Word Practice

Read the word.

find

Color the word.

find

Build the word.

i d f n

Clap !!!

How many syllables?

(1) (2) (3)

Trace the word.

find

Write the word.

Fill in the missing letters.

f_n_

Color the letters to make the word.

(n) (u) (f) (i) (n) (d)

(h) (x) (v) (w) (k) (z)

Find and circle the word.

your	when	find	what	find	other
find	find	write	were	them	find
down	about	some	find	from	each

 # Sight Word Practice 

Read the word.

long

Color the word.

long

Build the word.

n l g o

Clap !!!

How many syllables?

(1)   (2)   (3)

Trace the word.

long

Write the word.

Fill in the missing letters.

l__ __g

Color the letters to make the word.

(f) (u) (m) (b) (e) (r)

(h) (l) (o) (n) (g) (z)

Find and circle the word.

your	when	long	what	people	long
long	said	write	long	but	have
down	long	not	could	long	each

 # Sight Word Practice 

Read the word.

down

Color the word.

down

Build the word.

o   d   w   n

Clap !!!

How many syllables?

1   2   3

Trace the word.

down

Write the word.

Fill in the missing letters.

d_ _w_ _

Color the letters to make the word.

y   u   m   b   e   r

h   d   o   w   n   z

Find and circle the word.

your	when	first	down	people	down
come	down	write	were	down	have
down	about	down	could	from	each

 # Sight Word Practice 

Read the word.

day

Color the word.

day

Build the word.

a   y   d

Clap !!!

How many syllables?

(1)   (2)   (3)

Trace the word.

day

Write the word.

Fill in the missing letters.

d_ _

Color the letters to make the word.

(d) (a) (y) (b) (e) (r)

(h) (x) (v) (d) (a) (y)

Find and circle the word.

day	when	see	day	people	will
part	day	write	were	day	have
down	about	day	could	from	day

Sight Word Practice

Read the word.

did

Color the word.

did

Build the word.

d   d   i

Clap !!!

How many syllables?

1   2   3

Trace the word.

did

Write the word.

Fill in the missing letters.

d__ __

Color the letters to make the word.

d i d u e r

h x v d i d

Find and circle the word.

your	when	did	what	people	did
did	said	write	were	did	have
down	about	did	could	from	did

 Sight Word Practice 

Read the word.

get

Color the word.

get

Build the word.

e g t

Clap !!!

How many syllables?

(1) (2) (3)

Trace the word.

get

Write the word.

Fill in the missing letters.

g__ __

Color the letters to make the word.

(g) (e) (t) (b) (f) (r)

(h) (x) (v) (g) (e) (t)

Find and circle the word.

your	get	who	what	get	now
get	said	write	get	time	get
down	about	get	could	from	each

Sight Word Practice

Read the word.

come

Color the word.

come

Build the word.

o   e   c   m

Clap !!!

How many syllables?

1   2   3

Trace the word.

come

Write the word.

Fill in the missing letters.

c_m_

Color the letters to make the word.

n u c o m e
h x v w k z

Find and circle the word.

come	when	many	what	come	words
have	come	write	come	water	come
down	about	come	could	from	each

Sight Word Practice

Read the word.

made

Color the word.

Build the word.

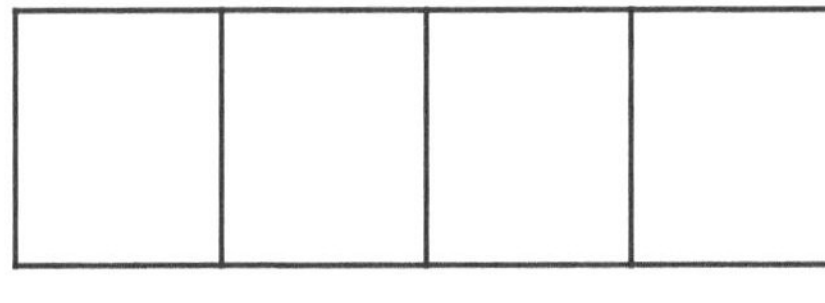

Clap !!!

How many syllables?

(1)   (2)   (3)

Trace the word.

Write the word.

Fill in the missing letters.

m__d__

Color the letters to make the word.

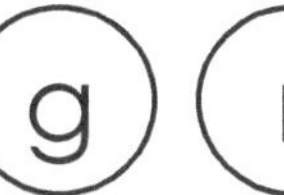

(n) (u) (y) (b) (g) (r)

(m) (a) (d) (e) (k) (z)

Find and circle the word.

your	made	look	what	made	each
made	said	write	made	first	have
down	about	made	could	from	made

Sight Word Practice

Read the word.

may

Color the word.

may

Build the word.

y a m

Clap !!!

How many syllables?

(1) (2) (3)

Trace the word.

may

Write the word.

Fill in the missing letters.

m__ __

Color the letters to make the word.

m a y b e r

h x v m a y

Find and circle the word.

may	when	many	may	people	part
number	may	write	were	may	have
down	about	may	could	from	may

 # Sight Word Practice 

Read the word.

part

Color the word.

part

Build the word.

r p a t

Clap !!!

How many syllables?

(1) (2) (3)

Trace the word.

part

Write the word.

Fill in the missing letters.

p__r__

Color the letters to make the word.

(f) (u) (m) (b) (e) (g)

(h) (p) (a) (r) (t) (z)

Find and circle the word.

your	when	part	what	people	part
part	said	write	part	more	have
down	part	their	could	part	each

Congratulations! You Did It!

Wow, what an incredible journey you've been on! Learning 100 sight words is no small feat, and you should be so proud of everything you've accomplished. You've worked hard, practiced daily, and now you're ready to take on even more reading and writing challenges. This is just the beginning of your amazing adventure with words!

Take a moment to celebrate all the progress you've made:

You've learned to recognize words at a glance.

You've practiced writing and tracing with care and precision.

You've developed your skills in spelling, building words, and solving puzzles.

Most importantly, you've grown more confident in your reading and writing abilities!

But remember, the journey doesn't end here. The skills you've gained from this book are tools that will help you in everything you do—reading books, writing stories, or simply exploring the world through words. Keep practicing the words you've learned, and don't be afraid to challenge yourself with new ones.

To parents and teachers:

Thank you for guiding and supporting this learning journey. Your encouragement and dedication have been key to this success. Keep fostering a love for reading and writing in your child—it's a gift that will last a lifetime.

To you, the amazing learner:

We are so proud of you! You've shown determination, focus, and creativity every step of the way. Remember, every word you learn opens new doors and takes you further on your path to becoming a confident reader and writer.

So what's next? Keep exploring! Keep creating! The world of words is full of endless possibilities, and we know you're ready to tackle them with excitement and curiosity.

Great job - you're a superstar! ☆